If I am not for myself,
who will be for me?
If I am not for others,
who am I for?
And if not now, when?

from The Talmud

HEALOGRAMS

SERIES
2

1. How To Feel Good In Relationships

2. How To Learn To Love Yourself

3. How To Boost Your Self-Esteem

4. How To Heal Your Inner Child

HEALOGRAMS

1

HOW TO FEEL GOOD IN RELATIONSHIPS

Bryan E. Robinson, Ph.D.
Jamey McCullers, R.N.

Health Communications, Inc.
Deerfield Beach, Florida

Publisher: Health Communications, Inc.
3201 S.W. 15th Street
Deerfield Beach, FL 33442-8190

Cover design by Andrea Perrine

How To Feel Good In Relationships

Most of us face the challenge of maintaining our self-esteem in relationships. We want to be close to others, yet we want to maintain a healthy sense of self too.

These *Healograms* — positive, healthy messages we send to ourselves — help us feel good about ourselves so that we can experience successful and fulfilling relationships. They help us distinguish healthy from addictive relationships and feel our own feelings, make

v

our own decisions and be our own person.

This booklet contains written *Healograms* on a variety of topics that can help you build your self-esteem. Reflect on each of the messages and silently apply it to your own life. Then become actively involved in the healing process as you write your own *Healograms*.

If you are a people-pleaser, if you are driven by "shoulds," "oughts" and other shame-based messages, if you put everyone else's needs before your own, if you are living your life for everyone but yourself, *Healograms* can help you take positive steps for a more fulfilling life. These affirming messages give direction to your life by guiding you through each day and reminding you to live with hope and optimism. They show you how to empower yourself and build up your self-esteem.

HEALOGRAMS

How To Feel Good In Relationships

Looking At The Whole Picture

Sometimes we zero in on our defeats and ignore our areas of achievement. For example, we may be successful in our relationships, careers and family but fall short in a tennis game. Then we berate ourselves and think of ourselves as failures because our tennis game isn't up to par. We allow one situation or person to determine our self-esteem, rather than see the whole picture.

All of us have the right to healthy self-esteem. When we enter a rose garden, we can be repelled by the thorns or drawn by the beauty and fragrance of the flowers. Let's ask ourselves, "Do I overlook my inner beauty and value because I focus on situations where I fall short?" As we begin to see ourselves honestly, the fragrance and beauty of our flower is more powerful than the pricking of its thorns.

When our self-esteem is low, we can ask ourselves if we're looking at the whole picture.

Attracting Healthy Relationships

We attract people and are attracted to people who reflect how we feel about ourselves. Some of us feel so badly about ourselves, we attract relationships which mirror our low self-esteem. We become dependent upon others for our self-esteem and all our emotional needs. If we dislike ourselves, we are attracted to others who dislike

themselves and express it in un-
kind ways. If we are not kind to
ourselves, chances are that our
friends and loved ones are not
kind to us either.

As we begin to heal our self-
esteem, we notice our relation-
ships change for the better. We
attract people (and are attracted
to people) who feel good about
themselves and who respect
themselves. We avoid relation-
ships with people who put us
down or minimize our worth and
seek out the company of those
who will affirm our true value.

As we begin to heal our self-esteem, we avoid relationships with people who put us down or minimize our worth and seek the company of those who affirm our true value.

3

Looking Within For Self-Esteem

How many of us look toward others to make us feel okay inside? Some of us believe that if we can just find Mr. or Ms Right, we will live happily ever after. We trick ourselves into thinking that another person will heal our low self-esteem. We look all around ourselves for that love and approval and continue to get involved in relationships that hurt us.

To heal low self-esteem we must let go of people-pleasing and blindly accepting other people's opinions of ourselves. The solution is to develop our own self-love. We need to stop beating ourselves up. We need to get to know ourselves and practice self-acceptance and self-approval. We concentrate on ourselves with self-nurturing thoughts, feelings and actions. We enjoy our own company and become our own best friend. We forgive, care for and support ourselves to the fullest.

*T*o heal low self-esteem we let go of gaining approval, people-pleasing and blindly accepting other people's opinions of ourselves.

4

Giving And Receiving

We get back from relationships what we put into them. We often enter relationships to get something from the other person. We may think we have nothing to give. Or we get so hung up on getting our own needs met, we become self-absorbed and ignore the needs of the other person. If we must give, we often do so grudgingly or in a self-sacrificial way because we equate giving with loss.

The truth is that when we give without being asked or expected to give, we get it back. If we want to be loved, we can love someone else and we get loved in return. As we give with all the love in our hearts, we experience feelings of love within us. In the process of giving our love away, we get it back.

When we give without being asked or expected to give, we get it back.

5

Keeping Our Individuality

All relationships are hard. Some are more difficult than others. One of the things that makes them so difficult is when we cannot tell whether the tension is coming from ourselves or the other person. Our boundaries are so blurred, we wonder, "Is it me or is it them?"

Many of us developed the habit of feeling others' feelings instead of our own. We haven't learned to have our own separate feelings. How many times do we test the mood of our spouse, children or loved one before we decide how we will feel?

To maintain our self-esteem in relationships we need to learn to feel our own feelings and to let others feel theirs. We recognize that we have a separate brain and heart. We can think and feel for ourselves. Getting in touch with our own feelings and feeling them teaches us to value them and to experience ourselves as unique and worthy.

Getting in touch with our feelings and feeling them teaches us to value them and to experience ourselves as unique and worthy.

6

Being
Somebody

Some of us spend our lives wishing we could be somebody. We need more money, a more prestigious job or a better relationship to reach "somebody status." Even songs, such as "You're Nobody 'Til Somebody Loves You," remind us that someone else can make us into a complete person.

To build our self-esteem we sing to the tune of a different song: "You're Somebody Whether Anybody Loves You Or Not." We already are somebody just the way we are without the trappings of worldly achievements and romantic relationships.

It is wonderful to be successful and prosperous and to have another person with whom to share our lives. But we do not need these conditions to have good self-esteem. Our value as a person begins within, through our own self-acceptance and self-love.

*O*ur value as a person begins within, through our own self-acceptance and self-love.

7

Giving Up
Mind-Reading

Can we read minds? No. Then why do we act as if we can? We meet someone new and after one evening out, they don't call again. Our conclusion? "I guess I'm not very interesting," or "I'm not attractive enough." Later we discover this person was sick in bed with the flu for a week and it had nothing whatsoever to do with us. But the damage to our self-esteem is already done.

Mind-reading is our way of filling in the blanks with our low self-esteem. When we start the mind-reading process, we can remember that it is a form of self-sabotage in which we put ourselves down. People do things because of *their* stuff — not ours. We can remind ourselves that we are still the same worthy and deserving person who has existed since the day we were born and who will exist until the day we die, regardless of the relationships in between.

We can give up mind-reading and fill in the blanks with messages that build our self-esteem instead of tearing it down.

8

Establishing Sound Friendships

How many of us compare our lives to those of friends or co-workers and wish we had the things they have? The grass always seems greener on the other side. When we constantly compare our lot to another's and feel cheated, we create a pit of low self-esteem. We judge ourselves unfairly when we use someone else's life as a yardstick to evaluate our own.

Comparing ourselves to everyone we know is a no-win situation because we always come out on the bottom. Winning comes from valuing and affirming our own gifts. We can look at the abundance around us, give thanks for what we do have and rejoice in our own uniqueness and talents. Establishing sound friendships comes from recognizing and believing in the value of our own lives, just as they are, and in applauding the good fortunes of others.

Establishing sound friendships comes from recognizing and believing in the value of our own lives, just as they are, and in applauding the good fortunes of others.

9

Expressing How We Feel

Many of us put our likes and desires behind those of others. As a result, our needs are never met. No matter how hard we try, there will always be someone who doesn't like or approve of something we do. We do not have to sacrifice our self-esteem in relationships just so others can have their way. Standing up for ourselves and voicing our point of view helps us feel good about ourselves.

We don't have to let another's discomfort cause us to back down. We are deserving and worthy, too. As we speak up and stand firm, we take care of ourselves and our self-worth grows. We discover that we like ourselves much better — and others do, too — when we express our feelings caringly with conviction and honesty. Expressing our ideas and feelings keeps our self-esteem intact and also allows us to keep ourselves open to other opinions.

We discover that we like ourselves much better — and others do, too — when we express our feelings caringly with conviction and honesty.

10

Empowering Ourselves In Relationships

Empowering relationships develop when two people love each other unconditionally, when both are strong and independent in knowing and appreciating who they are. But sometimes we victimize ourselves by living our lives for others and thinking of ourselves as helpless. We empower ourselves when we stop feeling the emotions that belong to others and begin to feel our own. We empower ourselves as we refrain from taking responsibility for others and become responsible for our own feelings and actions. We start feeling that we count for something and start standing up for ourselves.

It's not the situation that affects our self-esteem, but how we think, feel and act in the situation that makes the difference. It is time to start living our lives for ourselves instead of others and to take responsibility for healthy changes in our relationships.

It is time to start living our lives for ourselves and to take responsibility for healthy changes in our relationships.

11

Matching Our Insides
With Our Outsides

Are you an "innie" or an "out-ie"? Many of us tend to be *quantitative* successes and *qualitative* failures, successful on the outside and failing on the inside. We are accomplished when it comes to a measured success of "how much" and "how many," and have fat paychecks, accolades and trophies to quantify our success. But what about the qualitative life — how we feel deep inside?

We feel like failures as human beings because we sacrifice the inward quality of life to outward success. Success in the material world does not automatically guarantee positive self-esteem. Many of us already have our Ph.D.'s in *doing,* but to build our self-esteem, we need to work on our Ph.B's in *being.*

Examining our inner and outer lives helps us attain balance in both worlds so we experience success in its totality. If we fail in the business world, our inner success always picks us up.

12

Cleansing The Negativity

We are the victims of our own negativity — the only victims. When we hold on to negative feelings, we turn them inward upon ourselves where they do us emotional and physical harm.

When we feel negative toward ourselves or others, we can let it go, because holding on to it will keep us stuck in misery and despair. So our self-esteem increases as we refrain from negative thoughts and feelings.

Think of anyone (including yourself) you have condemned, criticized or treated unkindly — those whom you dislike, feel anger toward, resent or feel out of harmony with. Visualize letting go of your harmful feelings toward them until you feel cleansed. As we pull away from negative situations and create a positive frame of mind, we develop healthy relationships that mirror our own inner worth.

As we pull away from negative situations and create a positive frame of mind, we develop healthy relationships that mirror our own inner worth.

13

Overcoming Helplessness

We *always* have the power to choose how we think, feel and act, no matter how hopeless our lives seem to be. When we let other people or events make our decisions, we rob ourselves of self-esteem. We are not helpless pawns of fate, and no one else is responsible for how we feel or what we do.

We are responsible for our choices. As we increase our choices, our lives are enriched. We can look at the world with a better sense of balance, seeing its charm as well as its flaws. We can see blessings even in loss and disappointment. And we can *act* consistently with our thoughts and feelings, no matter how the relationship bends and sways.

We can act consistently with our thoughts and feelings, no matter how the relationship bends and sways.

14

Feeling Important

Many of us have been told through words or deeds that we are not important. Our self-esteem becomes paralyzed when we allow old thoughts to imprison us. We spend our lives figuring out what others want us to be like, and our interests and goals change to match those of the people we are with at the moment.

Feelings of importance come from within. We must believe we count for something. Once we feel that we are worthy of respect, people will start to treat us with respect. We can ask ourselves if we let relationships define our importance or if we work from the inside out? We can start feeling our importance by reminding ourselves of the following affirmation: *"I count for something, and I will feel and behave in accordance with this thought."*

I count for something, and I will feel and behave in accordance with this thought.

15

Reunion

Some of us have spent a lifetime looking outside ourselves for our self-esteem — through our jobs, relationships or gurus. We became caught up in controlling and changing other people to make them behave in a way that would make us happy.

Our self-esteem work must occur in our minds and hearts because the only way to change someone else is to change ourselves. All change takes place inside us, not in the outside world. It's time to come home to ourselves. Our reunion begins when we accept our own good and develop an intimate relationship with ourselves.

As we face ourselves, we realize this is the part of us that has been with us since birth and will be with us until the day we die. This is the self that stood by us even when we abandoned it — the self that has the potential to love us more than anyone on earth.

*O*ur self-esteem work must occur in our minds and hearts because the only way to change someone else is to change ourselves.